REMEMBERING OUR BLACK TRAILBLAZERS AND THEIR LEGACIES III

REMEMBERING OUR BLACK TRAILBLAZERS AND THEIR LEGACIES III

Barbara A. Pierce

Remembering Our Black Trailblazers and Their Legacies III by Barbara A. Pierce

ISBN 978-1-955136-37-2 (Paperback)
ISBN 978-1-955136-38-9 (Hardback)

This book is written to provide information and motivation to readers. Its purpose is not to render any type of psychological, legal, or professional advice of any kind. The content is the sole opinion and expression of the author, and not necessarily that of the publisher.

Copyright © 2022 by Barbara A. Pierce

All rights reserved. No part of this book may be reproduced, transmitted, or distributed in any form by any means, including, but not limited to, recording, photocopying, or taking screenshots of parts of the book, without prior written permission from the author or the publisher. Brief quotations for noncommercial purposes, such as book reviews, permitted by Fair Use of the U.S. Copyright Law, are allowed without written permissions, as long as such quotations do not cause damage to the book's commercial value. For permissions, write to the publisher, whose address is stated below.

Printed in the United States of America.

New Leaf Media, LLC
175 S. 3rd Street, Suite 200
Columbus, OH 43215
www.thenewleafmedia.com

DEDICATION AND ACKNOWLEDGEMENTS

Thanks to Barry Coleman for always being available to give his technical help when needed. And thanks to Jean Hurst and Beverly Pierce for their unwavering support.

Most images are from Wikipedia's public domain African-American historical photos with the exception of portraits of Barack Obama and Oprah Winfrey done by Maria Cole.

TABLE OF CONTENTS

Introduction			...1
Maya Angelou	1928–2014	Writer, Poet, Educator, Performer,	..3
Lorraine Hansberry	1930–1965	Playwright, activist	...5
James Forten, Sr.	1766–1842	Businessman, Abolitionist	...7
Oprah Winfrey	1954	Talk Show Host, Business Woman, Philanthropist, Actress	...9
Olivia Juliette Hooker	1915–2018	Educator, Psychologist, First Black American female in the U.S. Coast Guard	...11
Paul Leroy Robeson	1898–1976	Singer, Songwriter, Athlete, Civil Right Activist	...13
Alice Allison Dunnigan	1906–1983	Educator, White House Journalist	15
Malcolm X (Little)	1925–1965	Nationalist	...17
Katherine Dunham	1909–2006	Choreographer, activist	...19
Marcus Mosiah Garvey	1887–1935	Black Nationalist	...21
Asa Phillip Randolph	1889–1979	Professor, Lawyer, Labor Organizer	...23
Jesse Louis Jackson	1941	Minister, Civil Right Activist	...25
Leontyne Price	1927	Concert Opera Singer	...27
Clara McBride	1905–1992	Foster Parent, Childcare Advocate	29
Barack H. Obama, Jr.	1961	Senator, First African-American President	...31
Willie Mays	1931	Baseball Player, Philanthropist	...33

Name	Dates	Description	Page
Jacob Lawrence	1917–2000	Painter	35
Ella Fitzgerald	1918–1996	Jazz Singer	37
Charles H. Houston	1895–1950	Educator, Civil Rights Lawyer	39
Lena Horne	1917	Singer, Dancer, Movie Star	41
Jane Cooke Wright	1919–2013	Physician, Cancer Researcher	43
Claude Harvard	1911–1999	Teacher, Inventor	45
Charles B. Purvis	1842–1929	Surgeon, First Black Head of a Civilian Hospital	47
Shirley Ann Jackson	1946	Theoretical Physicist, Inventor	49
Francis L. Cardozo	1837–1903	Educator, Politician	51
Toni Morrison	1931–2019	Novelist	53
Colin Powell	1937–2021	Chairman of the Joint Chiefs of Staff, Four Star General	55
Stevie Wonder	1950	Musician, Singer, Songwriter, Activist	57
George W. Williams	1849–1891	Soldier, Lawyer, Politician, Journalist, Historian	59
Dorothy Vaughan	1910–2008	NASA Space Engineer, (Mathematician)	61
Mary W. Jackson	1921–2005	NASA Space Aeronautical Engineer (Scientist)	63
John Hope Franklin	1915–2009	Writer, Historian, Civil Right Activist	65
Muhammad Ali	1942–2021	Boxer, Civil Rights Activist	67
Angela Y. Davis	1944	Educator, Social Activist, Lecturer, Writer	69

Additional Research Recommendations 71

INTRODUCTION

    Remembering Our Black Trailblazers and Their Legacies III, is the third book of a series. It continues the same format as books I and II. A new set of thirty-four brief biographical sketches of extraordinary African-Americans whose struggles and successes paved the way to a more equitable future for all people. While a few may spark a bit of controversy, they are still a part of the American story. The accomplishments and legacies of each individual will be explored as you read further. At the end of the book there is a recommended list of individuals to research.

Hughes's Iconic 1922 Poem "Mother to Son"

> Well, son, I'll tell you:
> Life for me ain't been no crystal stair.
> It's had tacks in it,
> And splinters,
> And boards torn up,
> And places with no carpet on the floor_
> Bare.
> But all the time
> I'se been a-climbin' on,
> And reachin' landin's,
> And turnin' corners,
> And sometimes goin' in the dark
> Where there ain't been no light.
> So, boy, don't you turn back.
> Don't you set down on the steps
> 'Cause you finds it's kinder hard.
> Don't you fall now_
> For I'se still goin', honey,
> I'se still climbin'
> And life for me ain't been no crystal stair.
>
>   By Langston Hughes

Maya Angelou
Born: 1928
Died: 2014

MAYA ANGELOU

Maya Angelou was actually born Marguerite Annie Johnson in St. Louis, Missouri on April 4, 1928. She was the second child of Vivian and Bailey Johnson. Shortly after her birth the family moved to California, but the parents divorced when Maya was three. She and her brother Bailey Jr, were placed in the care of their paternal grandmother in Stamps, Arkansas. Unfortunately, when Maya visited her mother in St. Louis at seven, she was molested by her mother's boyfriend. After being arrested and later released the man was found murdered. The child thinking she had killed him with her voice when she spoke his name, became mute for five years. During those years, Maya became an avid reader and developed quite a passion for literature by writers such as Paul Laurence Dunbar, Langston Hughes, James Weldon Johnson, and W.E.B. Du Bois, though she could only read in silence. Finally, under the coaching of a woman name Mrs. Flowers, Maya completely regained her speech. She then returned to California to attend high school where she became deeply involved with drama, dance and literature. She was hired as a streetcar conductor in San Francisco, the first female ever to fill that role. Though she became a single teen mom, Maya continued to cultivate her skills. In 1952, Maya married Tosh Angelos, a Greek sailor. The union lasted two years. Again, to support herself and her son, Maya worked various jobs. In 1954, she scored a big break as a professional dancer in the international touring production of Porgy and Bess. Upon her return to the States, Maya Angelou chose New York where she sang in many clubs and at the Apollo Theater in Harlem. Becoming a member in the Harlem Writers Guild eventually resulted in her producing, directing and performing in Cabaret for Freedom, an Off-Broadway revue to benefit the Southern Christian Leadership Conference. She began her life as a civil rights activist when she agreed to replaced Bayard Ruskin as the northern coordinator for the SCLC under the leadership of Martin Luther King, Jr. who was on the forefront of the movement for racial equality. After a year, Maya left for Africa where she met and married her second husband Vusumzi Make, a South African freedom fighter. They moved to Cairo. The marriage ended when Maya against her husband's restrictions took a job as associate editor of the Arab Observer. Maya then moved to Ghana where she was hired as an administrator for the school of music and drama at the University of Ghana and as features editor for the African Review. Six years later, Maya returns to the U.S. to work with Malcolm X. Devastated by the news of his assassination, Maya experiences a withdrawal until Bailey intervened. Later, her friend novelist, James Baldwin encourages her to write her first autobiography, I Know Why the Caged Bird Sings (1970). It made literary history as the first nonfiction bestseller by an African American woman. Through the years she wrote numerous books of poetry and six additional autobiographies. She was Reynolds Professor of American Studies at Wake Forest University in Winston Salem, North Carolina. Maya also lectured and gave readings though out the world. One of her poems was delivered at the inauguration of President Bill Clinton. She was the only woman to speak at the Million Man March in1996. She passed in 2014 at age 86. Maya Angelou was a prolific writer, poet, teacher, civil rights activist, songwriter, singer, playwright, dancer, stage and screen producer, and actress. She was credited with a list of plays, movies, and television shows and received many honors over a span of fifty years.

Lorraine Hansberry
Born: 1930
Died: 1965

LORRAINE HANSBERRY

Lorraine Hansberry is best known for her popular play, A Raisin in the Sun. At twenty-nine, she was the youngest and the first African American whose work graced the Broadway stage, and won the New York Drama Critics Best Play of the Year Award in 1959. According to writer James Baldwin, "Never before in the entire history of the American theater has so much of the truth of black people's lives been seen on stage." The play's popularity grew nationally and the American theater changed forever. The play is a revelation of the complexity and suffering faced by a black family. It became an American classic after it was rejected twice for being too controversial, according to Columbia Pictures. Numerous musicals, film adaptations, and American television productions were made. The playwright was born in Chicago on May 19, 1930 to Nannie Perry Hansberry and Carl. Her middle-class up bringing was in the midst of the black freedom struggle. When Carl ran for Congress, and purchased a home in a white neighborhood near the University of Chicago, the family was attacked by an angry mob. The bricks hurled through their windows came close to injuring Lorraine. Such memories would influence her work later. The family filed a Supreme Court case against residential segregation, Hansberry v. Lee. It was a victory by the family, yet the racist real estate practices continued. After Lorraine studied literature for two years at the University of Wisconsin she moved to New York City to become associate editor of the radical black newspaper Freedom, founded by Paul Robeson. During her tenure as editor, Hansberry developed an involvement with the political, cultural, and artistic life of New York. In 1953 she married the progressive Jewish writer Robert Barron Nemiroff, and left the newspaper to pursue her own passion of writing. In 1963 Hansberry's second play, The Sign in Sidney Burstein's Window, was praised for its accurate characterizations of the Jew on the post-1945 stage. Nemiroff notes that Lorraine had a, "tremendous emotional identity with the Jewish radical and intellectual tradition." Diagnosed with cancer in 1963, the playwright fought the disease courageously while continuing her writing and civic involvement. Between treatment, she took charge of a fundraiser for the Student Non-violent Coordinating Committee. She led a walkout of a meeting with Robert Kennedy when he did not seem to understand what the black group of intellectuals were saying about civil rights. Though Lorraine and her husband divorced in 1964, he remained supportive and was her literary executor. After her death, Nemiroff adapted her unpublished writings for the stage as, To Be Young, Gifted and Black, a show that ran Off-Broadway in 1968-69 and toured college campuses in 1970-71. It is said Lorraine Hansberry was one of the most universal playwrights of her time. She died on January 12, 1965.

James Forten, Sr.
Born: 1766
Died: 1842

JAMES FORTEN, SR.

James Forten was born of free African-American parents in 1766. His birthplace was Philadelphia, Pennsylvania. At the age fifteen, Forten left his Quaker schooling to work aboard an American ship loading its cannons during the American Revolution. When the vessel was captured by the British, the youth was taken as a prisoner of war. His refusal to denounce his country for freedom resulted in him being detained for seven months. Upon his release before the end of the war in 1783, Forten chose to remain in England for a year. During that year he was introduced to the abolitionist philosophy. Once he returned to the U.S. he was apprenticed to Robert Bridges, a Philadelphia sailmaker. After years of being in the business of helping to make sails, he purchased the company after Bridges passed in 1798. Forten eventually, invented a device to make sails easier to work with on ships. During that era, sailing ships used sails, making his invention very popular. He became quite a prosperous businessman. By the 1888s as an activist in the abolitionist movement he supported the cause. He wrote in one of his noted pamphlets "A Series of Letters by a Man of Color" that opposed a Pennsylvania State bill that called for the restrictions of black emigration into the state. As a popular business owner, Forten was one of the strongest voices against the forced African-American colonization movement: the notion that freed slaves should be relocated to the African continent. The American Colonization Society, made up of primarily white slave owners attempted to pass legislation deporting all free African-Americans to Africa. Forten made a speech at the Bethel Church Congregation in Philadelphia reminding the audience that it was their ancestors that had enriched the soil with their blood and sweat. He encouraged them to remain in their new country and fight for freedom. He gained a great following in his community. His support did not end there. He pledged both his wealth and his name to his ideals and subsequently, founded the Pennsylvania Augustine Society to promote the education of people of color. Forten influenced William Lloyd Garrison a white abolitionist to use his newspaper, the Liberator to discourage the idea of such a movement. In exchange Forten provided funds and subscribers. Though Forten and both of his parents were born free, his grandparents were brought to America as slaves. He hated the demeaning and desperate positions slavery forced on helpless victims. So much of his wealth was used to help slaves. He never stopped fighting for the improved position of the African-Americans in America. James Forten became founder and president of the American Moral Reform Society and was active in the American Anti-Slavery Society. Many of his nine children followed in their father's footsteps and became abolitionists. The death of James Forten in 1842 was a real loss to the anti-slavery movement. Unfortunately, he didn't live to see the end of slavery, his words proved he never doubted it was coming: In his words, "The spirit of freedom is marching with rapid strides and causing tyrants to tremble…. May America awake…."

Oprah Winfrey
Born: 1954

OPRAH WINFREY

Oprah Winfrey is one of the most popular and successful entertainers in America. Her birthplace was Kosciusko, Mississippi on January 29, 1954. Her early childhood was often very harsh and lonely living with her overly strict grandmother who raised her until she turned six years old. Then she was sent to live with her mother in Milwaukee, Wisconsin until she became a teen and began to misbehave. Finally, Oprah was sent to live with her father and stepmother in Nashville, Tennessee. Her father kept tabs on her and her school progress. His strict but loving discipline kept her focused. Oprah did so well in school she won prizes for debating and giving speeches, and was popular enough to be elected class president in the senior year of high school. She entered a beauty pageant and won a full scholarship to Tennessee State College after catching the attention of a local radio station. Impressed by her poise and really great personality, she was hired by the station to read the news on the air. When offered a job on television as a news anchor in her freshmen year, Oprah accepted and chose to attend college in the day and work evenings. In 1976 she left the job for another anchor position at ABC in Baltimore that was not a good fit for her. Recognizing that fact, her producers tried her in the role of co-hosting the morning talk show. With great results, Oprah remained there until she left for Chicago as a talk-show host. She made book clubs across the country popular, and encouraged Americans to eat better, and exercise. She also made it okay for people to talk about their experiences and feelings. The show gained such a big following, it was renamed "The Oprah Winfrey Show" and was soon televised throughout the USA. After its twenty-fifth year run on network television, the show went to national syndication in 1986, making Oprah a very rich woman. But before the show went to syndication she had started other new projects. She acted in "The Color Purple" in 1965 and formed Harpo Productions in 1986, making her the first African-America woman to own a television and film studio. Other ventures that are credited to Oprah are the magazine (O); Network (OWN), a cable television network; and Oprah Radio, a channel on Sirius Satellite Radio; and through her Angel Network, help is extended to thousands of people globally, including the victims of natural disasters in need of rebuilding their lives. In 2004, Oprah became the first African-American woman among the fifty most generous people. She has donated more than 400 million dollars toward educational causes and more than 400 scholarships. Oprah is said to be the greatest African-American philanthropist in history. She was awarded the Presidential Medal of Freedom by Barack Obama and has received honorary doctorate degrees from Duke and Harvard Universities.

Olivia J. Hooker
Born: 1915
Died: 2018

OLIVIA J. HOOKER

Olivia J. Hooker was born in Muskogee, Oklahoma on February 12, 1915. That same year her parents, Samuel and Anita relocated the family to Greenwood, a middle-class district of Tulsa, Oklahoma often referred to as Black Wall Street. In 1921, the Hookers' relatively safe life, changed when the district erupted in a riot that claimed many lives and left scores of black owned businesses and homes destroyed. The attack was revenge prompted by a false rumor implicating a black neighborhood youth. Olivia was six when a lynch mob invaded and ransacked the family home during the "Tulsa Massacre of Black Wall Street". Mrs. Hooker hearing a disturbance and gun shots outside her home, rushes quickly to Olivia and her three siblings to hide them under a big covered oak dining table. From the vantage point of their hiding place, the children watched their valuable property being stolen and larger items hacked in pieces with an ax. Fortunately, because of the quick thinking of their mother, her family survived the horrors of the Tulsa Race Riot. Leaving Oklahoma, the family moved to Topeka, Kansas and later to Ohio where Olivia enters Ohio State University. In 1937 she became an elementary teacher after receiving her bachelor's degree. At the onset of World War II she became part of an initiative to get African-American women enlisted in the U.S. Navy. After being rejected, Olivia then tried the Coast Guard and became the first black woman in active duty and earned the rank of Yeoman Second Class. She served in the position until the women's reserve unit disbanded in 1946. Then Olivia went on to earn her master's degree in psychological services from Teacher's College at Columbia University in 1947, and in 1961 a doctorate in psychology at the University of Rochester. Dr. Hooker also served on the faculty of Fordham University from 1963 to 1985. Her focus was mainly those with developmental and intellectual disabilities. She helped found the American Psychological Association's Division 33 which serviced the needs of that population. Her life was spent serving others and being that tireless voice for justice and equality. On November 20, 2015, President Barack Obama recognized Dr. Hooker's Coast Guard service and legacy while in attendance at the 134th Commencement of the United States Coast Guard Academy. Dr. Olivia Hooker, one of the last known survivors of the Tulsa, Oklahoma Race Riot died November 21, 2018 at the age of 103 of natural causes in her home in White Plains, New York.

Paul Leroy Robeson
Born: 1898
Died: 1976

PAUL LEROY ROBESON

Paul L. Robeson was a gifted bass baritone singer whose concert performances captivated audiences worldwide during the twentieth century. He wrote some 276 distinct songs, acted on stage and also in motion pictures. He was well known for his political activism, and is noted as one of the first black artists to use his celebrity influence in support of the worldwide struggle against bigotry and injustice. Robeson was born in Princeton, New Jersey in 1898 to William Drew who escaped from slavery at fifteen, then later graduated from college eventually, becoming a Presbyterian minister. Paul's mother Maria Louisa Bustill perished in a house fire when he was six. Wanting Paul to excel academically, His father William enrolled him in a neighboring school system since Princeton was segregated and didn't offer secondary education to black students. In 1900, Willian resigned his position due to racial undertones from church supporters. The loss of sufficient income from the menial jobs he was forced to work, made it impossible to provide housing for himself and his children that were still home. Paul and his brother next to him were moved to the attic of a store in another town until their father was able to find a better situation. Once at St. Thomas A.M.E. Zion parsonage, Paul was able to cover for his father the times he was called away. In 1912, Paul attended Summerville High school where he excelled in sports and joined the school chorus. Often he had to ignore the racial taunts made by his white schoolmates. Paul won an academic scholarship to Rutgers College where he join the debating team and glee club on campus. He also sang off campus to earn spending money. Initially, his acceptance as a teammate on the football team was met with provocation because of his race. Eventually, He was twice named a consensus All-American in football, and graduated valedictorian. Unfortunately, William Robeson died earlier. While attending Columbia Law School in 1919-23 Paul Robeson played football in the NFL and got married. Paul chose acting over law after graduation. The talented vocalist soon developed a career in film and became a figure of the Harlem Renaissance after performing in the revival of O'Neill's The Emperor Jones, All God's Chillun Got Wings, and other popular classics. In the early 1930s after settling in London with his wife Eslanda, Robeson becomes aware of the sufferings of the British working class and the colonized peoples of the British Empire. He advocated for Republican forces during the Spanish Civil War and took an active part in the Council on African Affairs. On his return to the U.S. after a decade, he faced years of surveillance and harassment by the FBI because of his history of support for civil rights causes and pro-Soviet polices. Paul Robeson's career was destroyed because of his political beliefs.

Alice Allison Dunnigan
Born: 1906
Died: 1983

ALICE ALLISON DUNNIGAN

Alice Dunnigan was the first African-American female to break the barriers of sexism and segregation in the field of journalism. She later reveals her uphill struggle in pursuit of that profession in her autobiography entitled Alice A. Dunnigan: A Black Woman's Experience From School House to White House. Alice was born near Russellville, Kentucky on April 27, 1906 to sharecroppers Willie and Lena Allison Pittman who also took in laundry. Alice and her half-brother were brought up in a family that encouraged strong work ethics which fueled her dream of being a newspaper reporter. At thirteen, her journalism career began when she started writing brief items for the local Owensboro Enterprise paper. Unfortunately, only ten years of education was extended to students of Alice's race in the segregated school system. Her parents saw no benefit in more schooling for their daughter until the girl's Sunday school teacher intervened. Alice then chose to attend Kentucky Normal and Industrial Institute (now Kentucky State University) to enter in their teaching course. Alice becomes a history teacher in the Kentucky Public School System. Discovering her black students were unaware of contributions made by African-Americans to the nation prompted Alice to supplement their regular texts with fact sheets she developed. The fact sheets were later published in 1982 under the title, The Fascinating Story of Black Kentuckians: Their Heritage and Tradition. The meager wages in teaching forced her to migrate to Washington, D.C. during World War II for a government assignment. She attended night classes for a year at Howard University. Then in 1946, she was offered a job writing for The Chicago Defender, a black-owned weekly, as a Washington Correspondent. Her salary was much less than that of her male counterparts until she could prove her worth. Consequently, Alice had to take on additional writing projects to supplement her income. Finally, after being granted a press clearance, she became the first African-American woman to gain accreditation. She eventually rises to bureau chief of the Associated Negro Press for fourteen years before signing on as a White House Correspondent. In her book she mentions the racial indignities she endured as a correspondent at the White House. Nevertheless, Alice Dunnigan earned the reputation of being a hard-hitting reporter. She left the press galleries in 1960 to take a position on L.B. Johnson's Campaign for Democratic nomination. Though he did not win, Alice continued to be an important participant in many of the Party's initiatives until 1968. She received many journalism awards before her death in 1983, and was inducted in the Black Journalist Hall of Fame in 1985.

Malcolm X
Born: 1925
Died: 1965

MALCOLM X

Malcolm was born May 19, 1925 in Omaha, Nebraska to Earl and Louise Little. Earl moved his family often before settling in Lansing, Michigan believing it to be a safer environment for them after being bombarded with threats from the Ku Klux Klan. They soon found Lansing to be a violent place. Their home was firebombed, and in 1931 Malcolm's father, a Baptist preacher and active member of Marcus Garvey's Universal Negro Improvement Association was mysteriously found dead beside the local trolley tracks. Following her husband's death, Louise Little is eventually committed to a mental institution. Her younger children are split up and placed in foster care. Malcolm had already been removed from the home to foster care for juvenile delinquency, and made a ward of the State. He left school in eighth grade and accepted the invitation to live with a half-sister Ella and her husband in Roxbury, Boston a predominantly black section of Boston. Malcolm began his earlier years in Boston as a hustler, and later in Harlem. Known as "Detroit Red" and then "Big Red" as he was often called, found himself in trouble with the law for several criminal activities. His hustles came to an abrupt halt after he was arrested in 1946, and sentenced to seven years in the Charlestown, Massachusetts prison for burglary. Malcolm became a follower of Elijah Muhammad, leader of the Nation of Islam at the urging of Ella and brother Reginal. They suggested he change his "slave" name Little to X. Immersing himself in the study of the Bible, the Quran, and teachings of Elijah Muhammad. Malcolm, cultivated a new direction for his energies as he honed his oratory skills in prison debates and teaching other Blacks incarcerated. After parole in 1952, Malcolm X joined the Nation of Islam under the guidance of Elijah Mohammad leader of branches in Detroit, Chicago, and New York. He was assigned as the administrator and preeminent spokesman for the Muslim Nation. His role as spokesman was to preach the gospel of Islam: really as a racial spokesman. He soon becomes known as "the prophet of rage". In time he found his own mosques in Boston, Philadelphia, and in Harlem which expanded the movement and increased the membership upward of 30,000 members. A 1959 TV special with Mike Wallace called The "Hate That Hate Produced" told the story of Malcolm X's emergence as one of the most important leaders of the Nation of Islam. When his popularity began to overshadow his organizational allegiance, he acknowledged his debt to Elijah Muhammad. In 1963 Malcolm was silenced for 90 days after commenting on the assassination of President John F. Kennedy with the phrase "chickens come home to roost." 1963, Elijah Muhammad fearful that Malcolm X's power was out of hand, suspended him for ninety days. Discovering there were financial and personal improprieties that had been committed by Elijah, disillusioned Malcolm X. And learning there were plans to have him assassinated, he severed his ties with both the Nation of Islam and his formation of the Muslim Mosque, Inc. In 1964, he went on a pilgrimage to Mecca, as required of all Muslims, and changes his name to El-Hajj Malik El-Shabazz. Malcolm denounced Elijah Muhammad publicly, and becomes a Sunni Muslim, a more orthodox Islam that embraces an ideology that's inclusive of all races, still Malcolm did not abandon his black-nationalist stance. He still envisioned the need for building a black infrastructure within America. Unfortunately, Malcolm was assassinated while making a speech at the Audubon Ballroom in New York City on February 21, 1965. Three Black Muslims were convicted of the murder, though the Nation of Islam denied any involvement.

Katherine Dunham
Born: 1909
Died: 2006

KATHERINE DUNHAM

Katherine Dunham became one of the nation's most celebrated choreographers, and an activist for people of African heritage. She was born on June 22, 1909, near Chicago's South Side to Albert Dunham and Fanny June Taylor. Her mother died when she was quite young, and the family moved to Joliet, Illinois where Katherine developed a love for dance. While studying for her doctorate in cultural anthropology at the University of Chicago, her interest in black ethnic heritage grew especially in the Caribbean region. She would not accept that blacks were only capable of performing dance techniques to jazz and tap dancing to the exclusion of other forms. She often heard it said "blacks were made different and, couldn't do technical ballet." Katherine thought that was absurd. A dancer in her own right, she began to mix historical tradition with her creative approach to dance. After forming Ballet Negre with other dancers, she launched a career as one of the finest choreographers in America. Negro Rhapsody, their debut performance at the beaux Arts Ball in 1931, established Katherine as an expert on African dance styles, and she was chosen in 1933 to handpick 150 young dancers to perform a piece of her own design at the Chicago Century of Progress Exposition. Her work filled a void in American dance that had never been explored before. With the Rosenwald Travel Fellowship granted in 1935, Katherine traveled to the Caribbean to research if there were not dance movements and forms that were more associated with people of color, especially blacks. Traveling through Martinique, Jamaica, and, Trinidad and Haiti, Katherine observed up close some of the dances that African slaves brought to the New World. In the field of Haitian studies, she joined the small community of anthropologists whose interests ranged from Haitian peasantry religious rituals to their art and psychology. Katherine Dunham became one of the first African-Americans to appreciate the aesthetic beauty of vodou and its implication for dance anthropology. She was eventually initiated into its mysteries. Her Ballet Negre evolved into the Negro Dance Group and toured more than sixty foreign countries bringing her traditional African ritual to different nationalities in the form Caribbean inspired dance. Her choreographed pieces include Ballet Fedre (1938), Tropics and Le Jazz Hot (1940), Tropical Review (1943), Bal Negre (1946), Caribbean Rhapsody (1950), and Bamboche (1962). In 1946 Katherine wrote about her, Journey to Accompong, based on her fieldwork on the Free Maroon Settlement in the Jamaican mountains. The book examines the koromontee, a sacred, secret war dance and the myal dance, or dance of the dead. The information later influenced her choreography in other dance numbers. In the 1960s, she established the Katherine Dunham Center after retiring from the stage. Nevertheless, the dancer continued to train young people in African dance and culture. Always a supporter of African-inspired cultures, Dunham participated in a hunger strike in 1992 in support of Haitians who were denied asylum by the Bush Administration.

Marcus Mosiah Garvey
Born: 1887
Died: 1935

MARCUS MOSIAH GARVEY

Marcus Garvey was born in St. Ann's Bay, Jamaica in 1887. His mother was described as a soft-spoken devout Christian, and his father a bit distant but a well-read man of Maroon descent. His father was very influential in the foundation of his education. Marcus was the last of eleven children all of whom died during birth except, he and his sister, Indiana. Marcus quit school early to become an apprentice as a printer. Finally, he found a job as a printer and journalist in Kingston, and got involved in politics. At the age of twenty three he left the island and spent a few years traveling and working as a journalist, a printer, a publisher, and a timekeeper on the banana plantations of the Caribbean and Latin America. Disturbed by the oppressive conditions of black people he observed everywhere, prompted him to leave work on the plantations in an effort to find a solution to improve conditions for blacks. In time, Garvey left for London, where he gave street-corner lectures to expose the conditions of West Indians, and began writing for Duse Mohammed Ali's, Pan-African and Pan-Asian journal, the African Times and Orient Review. After reading Booker T. Washington's Up From Slavery, Garvey was inspired to return to Jamaica in 1914 with the idea he was born to lead blacks out of poverty and degradation. He founded the Universal Negro Improvement Association and African Communities League (UNIA), an organization that could protect blacks globally. Its motto was "One God! One Aim! One Destiny!" The UNIA would also act as a benevolent association with plans to build a technical college in Jamaica similar to that of Booker T. Washington's Tuskegee Institute. His vision changed when he found that the level of "race consciousness" among the black population of Jamaican was low, and they didn't see a need for such an organization. He left Jamaica hoping to interest Booker T. Washington in supporting his organization. After finding Washington had died a year earlier, he came to Harlem, New York in 1916. Following a short stay, he went on a five-month speaking tour throughout thirty-eight states. The excitement with Harlem and its large population of blacks was a catalyst for Garvey's return. From the street-corners of Harlem he preached his message of race pride and self-determination. His powerful oratory drew great crowds. In 1918, he set up a Harlem branch of the UNIA, and a year later branches in thirty other cities and recruited over a million members. He published The Negro World, a weekly paper which presented his views and information regarding the UNIA's activities. Garvey raised support to acquire the Black Star Line, a multiple ship company as a financial venture, and a future means of transport for those African-Americans consenting to go back to "the African Motherland." Garvey's popularity continued to soar when he established the Negro Factories Corporation. It developed a chain of businesses in Harlem that provided thousand jobs in the 1920s. Intellectuals and many ordinary people held reservations regarding Garvey's promises and plans, even though he now had millions of followers. In a month-long convention staged by Garvey in August 1920, hundreds of delegates from around the world attended his first convention. Its spectacular parade gave thousands of onlookers the feeling of great pride. The delegates to the convention were so impressed with the program, they voted to sponsor a free republic of Africa with Garvey as the leader. Before Garvey's ideals could be realized his Black Star Line went bankrupt and he was indicted for mail fraud. Once convicted he was sent to prison for two years in 1925 and later deported to Jamaica. Though he tried to make a come-back, he would never again enjoy the status of an international black statesman. In 1935, he succumbs to a second stroke in London, England.

Asa Phillip Randolph
Born: 1889
Died: 1979

ASA PHILLIP RANDOLPH

 Asa Phillip was a master strategist in the civil rights movement. He campaigned for economic equality. Known for his brilliant collective bargaining strategies, he became one of the nation's most successful African-American labor organizers. He was born and raised in Crescent Center, Florida in 1889. During high school he worked doing odd jobs in his father's tailor shop. After graduating valedictorian in 1907 from Cookman Institute, a segregated high school, he took on a series of menial jobs until he moved to New York in 1911. His aim was to pursue an education at City College and a career in acting. Jobs were in short supply, even in New York, so he settled for operating an elevator. Concern about the ill-treatment of those in menial jobs, Randolph organized a small union of elevator operators. His initial interests in acting were abandoned for a hands on political education in Harlem which was increasing with migrants from the rural South and the Caribbean. He became a frequent visitor of union halls and political rallies. After joining the Socialist party, Randolph later met a Columbia University student in 1914 who shared the same political views. At first the two men delivered their messages from the city's street corners. In 1917 they co-founded the, Messenger, a radical paper that published their controversial stands on the various topics of the time, such as urging African Americans to oppose America's entry into World War I. In 1925, Randolph was met with a bigger struggle for economic justice. His opposition was the Pullman Company, which ran the dining and sleeping cars on railroads across the nation. The company prided itself on its elegant black porters who performed acts of menial servitude for white customers. Requests for improve working conditions, rectified racist pay scale, and an opportunity for advancement had been ignored for years. Randolph's reputation as a fighter for economic justice led a group of the porters to ask him to represent them in their efforts. Thus the Brotherhood of Sleeping Car Porters was launched (BSCP). It was the first union of predominantly Black workers to be granted a charter by the American Federation of Labor. After Randolph's ten-year battle, his union won recognition as bargaining agent with the Pullman Company. Subsequently, his growing influence as a labor leader prompted him to fight for more opportunities for black workers nationwide. As president of the National Negro Congress, he was instrumental in persuading President Franklin D. Roosevelt to initiate the Fair Employment Practice committee. He was also elected a vice president of the AFL/CIO in 1957. In 1963 Randolph helped in the organizing of the March on Washington. In his later years he founded the A. Phillip Randolph Institute, a training and employment organization based in Harlem. He received the Presidential Medal of Freedom in 1964. Asa Randolph died in New York City on May 16, 1979.

Jesse Jackson
Born: 1941

JESSE JACKSON

Jesse Jackson a civil rights activist and a two-time candidate for the Democratic Party's presidential nomination. Jesse was born October 8, 1941 to Helen Burns a single teenage mom in Greenville, South Carolina. In 1959 he earned a football scholarship to enter the University of Illinois. After encountering racism on their football team, Jackson left there and enrolled at North Carolina Agricultural and Technical State College, a historically black school. Jackson became active in the civil rights movement while at the college. His leadership ability became more apparent as president of the student body. He was a fearless demonstrator, joining students protesting discrimination in local restaurants, libraries and other public places which often led to arrests. It was at that point he decided he wanted to pursue a career in the ministry. After graduating in 1964, Jackson got married to the former Jacqueline Brown, then subsequently entered the Chicago Theological Seminary at the University of Chicago in 1965. However, he would delay following through obtaining a degree for over thirty-five years. He chose to travel with a group of fellow seminarians to march with Martin Luther King, Jr., in Selma, Alabama. That was the beginning of his close association with King's Southern Christian Leadership Conference (SCLC). In 1966, King placed Jackson in charge of the Chicago branch of the Operation Breadbasket organization aimed at increasing the economic power and justice for African-Americans by securing steady jobs. Jackson, coming from a childhood of poverty himself, understood the needs of the disenfranchised. By 1967, he was the organization's national chairman because of his commitment. He was able to expand his Chicago-based program to finding jobs for African-Americans in every major city of the nation. Jesse Jackson left Operation Breadbasket in 1971 and founded PUSH (People United to Save Humanity), which was dedicated to increasing the economic power of African-Americans. PUSH became a forum to launch a variety of his programs from job training to voter registration. He ran his campaign for the Democratic nomination for the presidency in 1984 and 1988, though he had never held elective office. While he did not win, his run energized the black electorate, increasing voter registration among African-Americans. While Jesse Jackson's career as a candidate ended, he became a powerful behind-the-scenes presence in international politics helping to broker the release of hostages from Iraq in 1991, Bosnia in 1999, and Sierra Leone in 2000.

Leontyne Price
Born: 1927

LEONTYNE PRICE

Leontyne Price defied race, class and region to pursue a career in the musical arena of opera. She was born on February 10, 1927 in Laurel, Mississippi. James Price her father, was a carpenter, and her mother Katherine Baker Price was mid-wife. Leontyne exhibited musical talent as an infant and began piano lessons at three years old. As she grew older she sang in the church choir and often accompanied her mother on the piano. To earn a little pocket change she would sing at funerals and weddings. She gave her first recital on piano in high school during National Music Week in 1943. She played selections from Rachmaninoff, I. J. Paderewiski, and Tchaikovsky as well as "Bugle Boy Boogie" and "Deep River", her own arrangement. In 1944, Leontyne entered Wilberforce University a black college in Ohio where her talent was nurtured. She was encouraged to perform as much as possible and to change her major from music and education to voice. In 1948, her senior year, she was asked to sing on the same nearby program as Paul Robeson. Robeson was so empress with her talent, he offered her any assistance she needed to continue a career in music. Her professors aware that she wouldn't be able to afford any of the best music schools, set-up a Leontyne Price Fund for which Robeson gave a big fundraising concert. The concert raised one thousand dollars, and Leontyne was off to Juilliard School in New York. The City was very exciting and liberating for the new talent. She saw her first operatic performance, Puccini's Turandot, at the City Center. After a standing viewing of Salome at the Metropolitan Opera House, the new talent makes her decision to dedicate her life to opera. Her soprano voice was often described as being likened to the finest of violins. She was first introduced in 1955 in NBC's nationally televised dramatic and novel broadcast production of Giacomo Puccini's tragic melodrama Tosca. She was the first black woman to ever sing opera on television. Her sensual, graceful rendition of Floria Tosca, the principal character who eventually jumps to her death, was counted as a great historic moment. After Leontyne's stunning debut, she appeared in other major works in America and in Europe. A number of brilliant African-American opera singers began to perform during this period, but too often we lost them to Europe which recognized their talents beyond the color line. Eventually more African-American opera houses began to open, more opportunities were created for African-Americans in the operatic field. Leontyne's entrance on the national stage were during the years of heightened civil rights activity in the South. During that period she memorized Verdi's beautiful story of the Ethiopian slave, Aida, and performed the cunning Bess in George Gershwin's American classic, Porgy and Bess. She sang the leads in opera classics as varied as Madam Butterfly, La Boheme, Il Trovatore, Don Giovanni and Anthony and Cleopatra, which was written especially for her by her admirer Samuel Barber. Now having graced the stages at the Metropolitan, the San Francisco Opera Company, the Lyric Opera of Chicago, and the major European opera venues, she chose to do less grand performances and concentrate on concert recitals and recordings to expose a larger, more popular audiences to the gravity and grace of opera.

Clara McBride Hale
Born: 1905
Died: 1992

CLARA McBRIDE HALE

Clara McBride founded the Hale House which was the first program in the United States for drug addicted-babies. "Mother" as she was called, dedicated her life to caring for abandoned, neglected and abused children. She was born in Elizabeth City, North Carolina, but raised in Philadelphia, Pennsylvania. When Clara was nine her father was lynched by a white mob. Then as the sole support of the family, her mother took in boarders and ran a lunch room. After high school, Clara got married and moved to New York City. Her husband ran his own business and took courses at City College. Clara became a domestic and cleaned movie theaters. Unfortunately, Clara's husband after a diagnoses of cancer, lost his battle when she was twenty-seven. Left a young single parent with three small, children, she made her home a neighborhood daycare that took care of her family needs as well as her neighbors. Clara eventually got a license and became a foster parent. She raised forty foster children between 1941 until her retirement in 1968. Clara's retirement ended in 1969, the day her daughter brought home a young addict she found slumped over in a stupor clutching an infant in her arms. After the word of Clara's act of benevolence hit the streets, three weeks later, she had twenty-two more to care for in her five-room apartment. They had been either dropped off by their mothers or just simply left on the doorsteps. All of the children were suffering from heroin withdrawal and required constant care. Initially, she was dependent on the support of her children and her neighbors who donated money, food, clothing and time as well. Then Clara was awarded a $50,000 grant from the Office of Economic Opportunity. In 1973, her charity was incorporated as Hale House Center for the Promotion of Human Potential, Inc. The Borough President assisted in the new Hale House Center's relocation to a large brownstone that accommodated all of her needs. In the 1980s, the number of neglected and abandoned children increased considerably due to the aids epidemic and an increase of drug consumption. Though it took more time to access the special needs of the HIV-positive and addicted babies, Clara's fundamental philosophy remained the same. In her own words, "We hold them and rock them. They love you to tell them how great they are, how good they are. Somehow, even at that young age, they understand that. They're happy, and they turn out well." And since their ultimate goal was to repair and reunite families when possible, programs were developed to help drug-addicted and HIV-positive parents also. Over her fifty years of service to the Harlem community, Mother Hale improved the lives of over a thousand children and their families. Her selflessness brought national attention to the devastating effects of poverty and drugs on the urban family. In 1985, Mother Hale was recognized by President Ronald Reagan in his State of the Union Address calling her "a true American Hero." Clara responds to others "I'm not an American hero, I'm simply a person who loves children." Clara McBride known to most as "Mother Hale" passed away in 1992.

Barack Obama, Jr.
Born: 1961

30 | BARBARA A. PIERCE

BARACK OBAMA, JR.

Barack Obama became the first African-America elected to the presidency of the United States. He served two terms. He was born in Hawaii to white teen mother Ann and an African student Obama, Sr. from Kenya in 1961. After receiving an offer of graduate work at Harvard, Obama, Sr. left the family with in-laws in Hawaii only to return eight years later, shortly before his death. The boy, too young to know the situation, enjoys living with his mother and grandparents who calls him Barry. In 1967, Ann married Lolo Soetoro, who moved the family to his home Jakarta, Indonesian. Lolo treats Barry as his own son. When Barry came home with a wound on his head one day, after hearing his story, Lolo told him that a young man should be able to defend himself. He gave the boy gloves and taught him to box. He told Barry that he had learned being strong could mean power and protection. And if you can't be strong, be clever and make peace with someone who is strong. But it's always better to be strong yourself. A lot of his time spent in Indonesia was joyous and full of adventure and mystery. When the family income grew they moved to a bigger home with a few more luxuries such as a refrigerator and a television. In 1970, a new baby named Maya was born. Barry wrote to his grandparents often, but never told them about any of the upsetting things he witnessed. Not everyone was as fortunate as his family. Beggars often come to their door asking for food. Even having a job in Indonesia was no guarantee against poverty. Barry saw how famers suffered if their crops ruined during seasons with too much, or too little rain. Just as tragic, was the downpour of rain that flooded streets, cause havoc to barns and homes, and endanger livestock. Dissatisfied with the education Barry got in local schools, Ann gave him extra English lessons for three hours each morning before leaving. He often protested, but she was persistent and felt he needed to be able to read and write English as well as any boy raised in the States. Realizing even with her help, none of the opportunities in Indonesia would ever be as broad as they could be in America. Ten year-old Barry Obama won a scholarship to go to the exclusive Punahou School for bright children. He lived with his grandparents in a two-bedroom apartment. The boy was quite nervous his first day not knowing any one there. And being asked if his dad in Kenya was a cannibal, did not help. No one at the school played soccer or badminton, the sports he knew, and he didn't know how to ride a skateboard or play football as his classmates did. Ann had completed her graduate work when Barry turned sixteen, she made plans to return to Indonesian with her children to do her field work. Barry had already gotten permission to stay again with her parents, if he did not cause any trouble. Being a typical teenager, he went through the same awkward teenage stages as everyone else he knew. In the next few years he took refuge on the basketball court and went on to play for his Punahou high-school team. Obama wrote in his book, Dreams From My Father that adolescence in Hawaii was difficult. He wrote that he "learned to slip back and forth between my black and white worlds," He was sure his family love him, but he felt "totally alone." In 1979, Obama graduated from Punahou High and entered Occidental College in Los Angeles, California where he took part pressing the College to pull its money out of South Africa. Barak found he liked political action, and was good at it. He transfers to Columbia in 1981 in New York City, majoring in political science. In 1983, Barack began his first job as a researcher. In the summer of 1988, Barack visited his father's homeland before entering Harvard Law school, where he also becomes the first African-American president of the Harvard Law Review. Barack Graduates from law school in 1991 and moves back to Chicago as a civil rights Lawyer and marries Michelle Robinson in 1992. A few policies implemented during the Obama Administration: health care reform, student loan reform, and an economic stimulus bill, loans to automakers to stimulate jobs, etc.

Willie Mays
Born: 1931

WILLIE MAYS

Willie Mays was the leading talent in the National League in 1954. His amazing knack for making one catch after another also made him the hottest. His fans were awed by his dance-like movements across the field. Some say Willie Mays was one of the most exciting center fielders of the day. He represented the fun of the sport and transformed it into an art. Willie Mays was born in 1931 during the Depression in Westfield, a steel mill town in Alabama. His parents were divorced, and he was sent to live with his aunt in Fairfield, Alabama. At sixteen, he joined his father's semipro baseball team, the Birmingham Black Barons of the Negro National League sponsored by the steel mill where his father worked. After graduation from high school in 1950, four years after Jackie Robinson broke the color line, the Giants signed Willie Mays to join their minor league affiliate. After playing in Trenton and Minneapolis his first year, Willie Mays develops a fear of failure which he reminisces about in his autobiography, Say Hey. His manager Leo Durocher convinced him to remain with the team. Fortunately Mays, stayed despite the Giants' World Series loss to the Yankees, Mays ended his first season with 20 home runs, 68 runs batted in. He was named Rookie of the Year. Mays fought in the Korean War between 1951 and 1952 for a time. In his absence the Giants finished second in 1952 and third in 1953. When he returned to the Giants in 1954, they succeed in winning the pennant beating the Cleveland Indians in the World Series. Willie Mays played center field twenty-one years for the team in New York, 1951-1952, 1954-1957 and later in San Francisco, 1958-1971. Then in 1972 he was traded to the New York Mets. In 1973 Mays retired from the game. As the Most Valuable Player who helped the Giants win the World Series in 1954 and who played in every All-Star game from 1954 until 1973, Mays was New York's number one son. In the mid-sixties he was the best outfielder in the major leagues. He led the league in stolen bases in four consecutive years. His total home runs were (660), the third-highest all-time record, behind Hank Aaron with (755), and Babe Ruth with (714). Mays had also made a total of 3,283 hits and a life time batting average of .302. He was elected in the Hall of Fame in 1979, the ninth player in history to get in on the first try. At his ceremony he said, "What can I say? This country is made up of a great many things. You can grow up to be what you want. I chose baseball, and I loved every minute of it. I give you one word__ love. It means dedication." Mays brought his own distinctive style to baseball, a style that put great value at being himself at all cost, a genuine honesty mixed with fun, talent, and irrepressible love. He started a foundation to help poor adults and children financed by the golf tournament he ran yearly in Briarcliff, Manor, New York while serving as a special assistant to the president of the Giants organization.

Jacob Lawrence
Born: 1917
Died: 2000

JACOB LAWRENCE

Jacob Lawrence was a prolific African-American artist of the thirties. He used brilliant colors of paints from limited medium of flat tempera, and transform formless designs into living, moving shapes to bring the history of black life alive in his paintings. His art memorialized the tragedy, the aspirations, the struggle, and the joy of everyday African-Americans. Often, in his paintings he incorporated sweeping narratives of the experiences of forgotten or ordinary folk. Depression-stricken Harlem influenced his artistry. He adeptly depict the social changes of the great migration as African-Americas moved to the industrialized cities in the North. The fact he was able to register in his paintings such a monumental change in the visual realm was a great achievement. In the 1930s, Black artists embraced progressive and working class themes, however he admired the images by varied artists as the Mexican muralist Clemente Orozco; the European social realist artist such as Kathe Kollowitz, William Gropper, and George Grosz; and the Chinese woodcut artist. Jacob Lawrence integrated his technique with his thematic passion for creating a visual narrative of black history. He painted panels that he called his Migration series. The first reads, "During the war there was a great migration by southern Negroes." Jacob and his parents are portrayed among the nameless, faceless shadows of these paintings. As the series continue, the text recall the railway trains movement: " And still they came," as black migrants arrived in New York, Chicago, St. Louis, Philadelphia and other northern cities, fled southern poverty and racism, etc. Jacob Lawrence was born in New Jersey September 7, 1917. When his parents split-up, his mother took her children to Harlem, where she enrolled him in the WPA-sponsored after-school art classes at Utopia House, where the painter Charles Alston was giving arts and crafts classes at the New York Public Library. At nineteen, Jacob began to study at Alston's Workshop in Harlem and the American Art School where he was given a two-year tuition scholarship. He studied among a few notable artists. The sculptor August Savage took an interest in his work and arranged for his employment at the Federal Arts Project. In part of the program Jacob was given the opportunity to practice his art full-time. He grew as an artist while working in the project divisions of the program. The regular exchange of ideas in an atmosphere with black and white artists on the verge of success abound with creative electricity. Jacob often said this period was formative for him and that it fertilized his aesthetic vision. In 1937, Jacob began to work on his second series based on the life of Toussaint L'Ouverture, the liberator of Haiti. "I've always been interested in history," Lawrence once said. "but they never taught Negro history in the public school…. It was never studied seriously like other subjects." Black history clubs flourished in Harlem after several of Lawrence's black historical theme paintings were dedicated. No artist before Jacob had developed themes from African-American history. He was busier throughout the 1970s than ever. Before his death on June 6, 2000, Jacob Lawrence had received many honors for his lifetime of artistic contributions. In 1990, he received the National Medal of art. In 1994, he was inducted into the American Academy of Arts and Letters. He is admired for being the first black visual artist to make the African-American historical traditions the subject matter of his art. (The following is a short-list of more of his artistic renderings. The Harlem Series collection, the Frederick Douglass Series, the Harriet Tubman Series, the George Washington Bush Series, the Builders Series etc.)

Ella Fitzgerald
Born: 1918
Died: 1996

ELLA FITZGERALD

Ella Fitzgerald was the most popular female jazz vocalist in America for more than fifty years. She was born in Newport News, Virginia in 1918. Her mother moved the family to Yonkers, New York after the death of her husband. Ella's career unexpectedly developed after friends dared her to enter an amateur contest. Accepting their challenge, her intent was to dance, but feeling too weak, she started singing, "The Object of My Affection." Ella won first prize and by popular demand, was requested to sing three encores. After that, she entered and won many more talent competitions. In 1935, Ella was heard at the Apollo Theater and days later was given and audition by the band director, Chick Webb who hired her that day. At seventeen Ella Fitzgerald began singing with Chick Webb's band at the Savoy Ballroom. When she developed a case of stage-fright Webb encouraged her to "listen to the beat and relax; go with the beat, always go with the beat." Soon, Ella was back on track with her silky flawless notes into and around the rhythm. She cut her first record, " Love and Kisses " in 1935. She then began to try out her talent of imitating musical instruments and developed her spontaneous " scati " style only she was known to use. After using it for the first time in " Mr. Paganini " or " If You Can't Sing It, You'll Have To Swing It " in (1936), It became Ella Fitzgerald's signature. That style brought perfection in live recordings of " How High the Moon " (1960) and " Mack the Knife " (1960). Her first smash hit, " A Tisket , A Tasket she co-wrote with Webb's group in 1938 sold over a million recordings sent to the top. Ella was now in the national spotlight, and she continued to compose as well as record hits. She wrote lyrics for songs performed by Billie Holiday and Duke Ellington, and the youngest person to ever join the American Society of Composers, Authors and Publishers in 1943. From 1948 to the early fifties Ella Fitzgerald took part in the regal jazz performances at the Philharmonic tours organized by Norman Granz who became her manager and producer in 1954. During her long partnership with Granz, Ella became one of the most successful singers in the world. Ella Fitzgerald's sublime singing earned her the title "the First Lady of Song."

Charles Hamilton Houston
Born: 1895
Died: 1950

CHARLES HAMILTON HOUSTON

Charles Hamilton Houston was one of the giants in the legal fight for racial equality. Though he was not as well known as his protégé Thurgood Marshall, or the victories he'd had including the 1954 case of the (Brown vs Board of Education) Supreme Court decision that ended legalized segregation in all public education. Houston never appeared phased by the lack of public acclaim received for his leadership. He continued to perform duties and life with a steady, calm energy and brilliance that drew attention to his skillful legal arguments, rather than himself. Houston often told his Howard Law students, " Lose your temper, you lose your case." Houston was born September 3, 1895, and raised in Washington, D.C. The family placed great value on getting an education. As a school age child, Houston was place in top schools in Washington, D.C. After excelling at the prestigious M Street School in 1911, he enrolled at Amherst College, an all-white school. Being the only black student in the class did not affect his studies; he graduated in 1915 and was elected to Phi Beta Kappa. Houston took a part-time teaching position at Howard University, but left in 1917 to enter World War I. Though he was opposed to the army's racist practices of segregation, he wanted to advocate for a separate training program for black officers. He felt that was how he could contribute his talent to his country at war. Houston trained at an all-black officers' school in Iowa, and in 1918 he was shipped to France as a second lieutenant in the segregated army. After the negative reception received from his fellow American officers, Houston felt it did not make sense to give his life for a world ruled by them. He made up his mind if he survived that war, he would study law and advocate for men who could not strike back. He kept his promise and entered Harvard Law School in 1919, and was the first black student to edit the law review at Harvard. Houston graduated in 1922, he went to Madrid, Spain for additional legal study. On his return, he worked in his father's law firm until 1929, when he joined the law school at Howard University as its vice dean. During Houston's administration the school earned its accreditation and became a training ground for lawyers interested in litigation against racism. Houston not only shared his expertise at the Law School, he crisscrossed the southern states with NAACP's secretary Walter F. White, documenting the racial inequality and planning legal strategies to fight it in the 1930s. He was encouraged in 1935 to join the NAACP as its first chief counsel. His was hired to focus on educational equality, but he also represented criminal defendants and successfully argued against the exclusion of African Americans from juries (Hollins v. Oklahoma, 1935) before the Supreme Court. When Houston's health began to fail, he left the job in the hands of Thurgood Marshall, his protégé. Returning to his father's firm, he took on two unions in labor cases that reached the Supreme Court. In 1944 he joined the Fair Employment Practice Commission. In 1948 he argued his last case before the Supreme Court which struck down the Legal enforcement of racially restrictive real estate covenants (Shelley v. Kraemer). Charles Houston died in 1950. Thurgood Marshall eulogized Houston as "the engineer of it all."

Lena Horne
Born: 1917

LENA HORNE

Singer, actress, and legendary beauty, Lena was born June 30, 1917 in Brooklyn, New York. Her parents divorced while she was a toddler. To find work as an actress, her mother left her with the grandparents. Lena's mother came back for her when she was seven years old. The rest of her childhood was spent moving from place to place with her mother in pursuit of an unsuccessful acting career. Short periods of time, Lena attended schools in Florida, Georgia, and Ohio. At fourteen she quit school and later returned to Brooklyn where she got her first stage job dancing. At sixteen, she started as a chorus dancer at the famed Cotton Club in Harlem. The exhausting job was not glamorous or well paid. Aware that she was hired for her good looks, Lena passionately pursued singing lessons on her own time. She was taken under the wings of more seasoned artists such as Duke Ellington and Cab Calloway, to help her over rough spots in show business. Before long, the sultry voice that she is known for began to take shape. Encouraged by Duke Ellington and friend Billy Strayhorn, Lena moved forward with her singing career. Before long Lena was playing before packed houses. In the mid-1930s she left the Cotton Club to sing and tour with Noble Sissle's Society Orchestra, based in Philadelphia. In 1934, Lena played in her first Broadway show, a musical and her first movie which were both unsuccessful. Fortunately, better work came along. In 1939, she was cast in Lew Leslie's Blackbirds, and not long after, saxophonist Charlie Barnett's all-white band hired her to sing as their lead. Before the outbreak of World War II, Lena made her first record with clarinetist Artie Shaw and trumpeter Henry Allen. Lena suddenly becomes a legend in Hollywood. Unfortunately, after signing on with MGM her movies were shot so her scenes could be cut out when they were shown in the South. During those years, the South had ridiculous notions about race. Movie executives had fears of losing revenue if a black performer played in a role other than as a servant or other minor occupation. She rejected stereo-typed roles. In 1943, MGM loaned Lena to Fox Studios for the role of Selina Rogers in the all-black musical, Stormy Weather. It became a big hit and so did the song, Stormy Weather. In 1943, Lena appeared in Cabin In The Sky, which is regarded as one of the finest performances of her career.

Jane Cooke Wright
Born: 1919
Died: 2013

JANE COOKE WRIGHT

Jane Cooke Wright a third generation physician in her family, was born to Dr. Louis and Corinne Wright November 30, 1919 in New York City. Her mother was an elementary school teacher and her father was a well-respected surgeon at Harlem Hospital, the first African-American on staff. Jane grew up observing her fathers' path to success and the impact it had on others. While attending the City's Ethical Culture School and Fieldston High School, Jane decided to attend college and make a difference also. After she graduated high school in 1938, she was accepted at Smith College in Massachusetts known to cater to the wealthy and gifted students. There was no lack of confidence on her part, the curriculum demands of her high school and her excellent study skills prepared her to compete. Jane felt she was ready for the challenge. The only difficulty she faced was in selecting a major. Every subject had some excitement for her, but by the end of her sophomore year, her choice is physics and she decides to pursue medicine. As a member of the college varsity swim team, Jane set records that last for many years. She graduated with highest honors in 1942. She passed her comprehensive examinations in seven subjects with highest distinction. She now was prepared to follow in the footsteps of her father, as he followed in those of his father. Jane found her father to be a great mentor who was able to make the world of medicine and research easier to understand. He showed how to successfully test for childhood diseases. Watching her father working with patients in the hospital, Jane discovers the importance of caring for other people. In 1942, Jane wanted to enroll at Harvard but, women were not accepted. When she was awarded a four-year scholarship to the New York Medical College, it meant a lot to her now. Her father was ailing with severe lung damage he sustained during an enemy gas attack in World War I and had tuberculosis. While it did cause some financial hardship for the family, Jane's mother encouraged her to finish her education. After medical school Jane completed her internship in internal medicine at Bellevue Hospital and two residencies at Harlem Hospital. Along the way Jane got married and had a family. In 1948, a year after his daughter's marriage Dr. Louis Wright established the Cancer Research Foundation to study Chemotherapy treatments at Harlem Hospital with the support of grants from the National Cancer Institute and another funder. Dr. Jane Wright joined her father in his pioneering research. This gave her an opportunity to learn about the innovations in cancer treatment. Before the 1940s treatment included unsuccessful remedies that caused more pain for the patients. Her new mission was to find a more effective treatment. Funding for chemotherapy research was difficult, but through National Institutes of Health, the National Cancer Center, and the United States Public Health Center the federal government provided much of the support for Dr. Wright's research. In 1952, Dr. Louis Wright suffered a heart attack and died. Dr. Jane Wright continued her work at New York University as a professor of research surgery and the director of chemotherapy. During the 1950s and 1960s she treated cancer patients with various types of anti-cancer drugs gaining more knowledge and experience with new treatments that prolonged her patient's lives. Still Dr. Wright hoped to find a way to help her patients with cancer live even longer. Dr. Wright following in her father's footsteps, found her own path. She published 135 papers and made contributions to nine books. She was one of the seven founding members of the American Society of Clinical Oncology, and the first woman elected president of the New York Cancer Society. She also was the first African-American woman to become a dean of a medical college, New York Medical College. Dr. Wright's concern for others gave her a reason to travel the world to present the latest knowledge in cancer research and treatment.

Claude Harvard
Born: 1911
Died: 1999

CLAUDE HARVARD

Claude Harvard's biggest dream at nine years old was to own a wireless radio set. Since his parents were sharecroppers in Dublin, Georgia, Claude knew getting a set was very slim. And their town didn't have a radio station. Nevertheless, his dream remained. He had the good fortune to come across a magazine with an article entitled, "Have Your Own Wireless Radio Set". The idea of owning his own set was so exciting, Claude figured a way to make the money needed to purchase one. He tuned into the nearby Atlanta station. When he was eleven, the family moved to Detroit, Michigan. Of course, he took the wireless radio set. In Detroit, the boy's machine shop teacher noticed his interest in electronics and machines and told Claude about the Ford Trade School. Henry Ford, the auto magnate had started the school to train orphans to do a specific job for his company. Even though Claude was not an orphan he applied hoping it would a good opportunity him. The principal was so impressed with him, he made an exception to the rule. Claude received an acceptance letter. Claude had learned everything there was to know about automobiles by the age sixteen. He joined a radio club, and the other members elected him president. Out of the ten members taking the test for local certification, Harvard was the only one that passed. He became the first African-America in Michigan to receive an amateur radio operator's license. On the air at the Ford Trade School station, WARC, he called himself the "African Pounder." Though he graduated at the top of his class, and had invented a device patented in the school's name, Harvard was overlooked when other students were automatically given union cards. He figured it to be an oversight, but he was never issued one even after it was brought to the administration's attention. Years later, he was informed the union had thrown out his applications. The Ford Company created a new job to use his talent. He became head of a radio department. During his employment with the company, Claude Harvard invented more than twenty-six devices patented by the Ford Motor Company. Ford even sold one of his inventions to the United States Steel Company for $250,000. The patents for Claude Harvard's inventions were assigned to the Ford Motor Company, because their employees had to surrender their rights to anything they invented while on the job. At twenty-three, Claude was asked by Henry Ford to demonstrate another of his inventions, an automated piston pin inspection machine during the 1934 Chicago, Illinois Century of Progress Exposition. Ford was pleased with Claude's work at the fair, he had Claude prepare a speech for him to deliver the following day at the Tuskegee Institute. Since Claude knew very little about the school, he did research at the library about the school and on how to write speeches. When he return with the speech, Ford praised the thorough job he had done, because Clause himself would be representing him at Tuskegee. Claude Harvard got the rare opportunity to meet the famous scientist, George Washington Carver, who was almost eighty years old. He got the chance to tour Carver's laboratory and see some of his fascinating inventions. Despite his success at Ford Motors, Claude wanted to see how far he could go on his own as an entrepreneur, he opened a tool and general design company. The business flourished until white employees of customer companies discovered he was black, and refused to work with him. Harvard, thought that working for the federal government would be an equal opportunity job. Again he faced disappointment finding his white co-workers with no knowledge of machinery were paid higher wages than he. His luck changes after a friend he knew from the Ford Trade School spoke to his supervisor about Claude's ability. After he was given a problem in trigonometry which he answered it in seconds, he took a civil service examination that he passed with flying colors. Life was not always fair to Claude Harvard "If it had not been for ingenuity" he said, "I would have suffered. Today, I am retired on an engineer's pension." A number of his inventions have revolutionized automobile manufacturing. He loved the joy of teaching science and the art of invention.

Charles B. Purvis
Born: 1842
Died: 1929

CHARLES B. PURVIS

Charles B. Purvis dedicated a good part of his adult life working to improve the medical care for black Americans in the South. His concern was with the reality of the death rate for blacks in many Southern communities were routinely higher than whites. One-quarter to one-third of former slaves had died by the mid-1830s. Purvis assumed the task of training black doctors to care for their people. Charles Purvis was born in 1842 to Harriet Forten, daughter of abolitionist, inventor, and businessman James Forten, Sr. and Robert Purvis, Sr. the wealthy abolitionist and civil rights leader. Purvis received early schooling in Quaker schools in Bayberry, Pennsylvania. He also learned a lot from prominent anti-slavery leaders that visited his family home. He was enrolled at Oberlin College in Ohio from 1860 to 1863. Then he enrolled in Wooster Medical College (renamed Western Reserve Medical School) in Cleveland. During the summer of 1864, Purvis worked as a military nurse at Camp Barker where he saw firsthand how desperately ex-slaves needed medical care. He graduated from Wooster Medical College in 1865. He enlisted in the Union army as an acting assistant surgeon. He served in the army from 1865 to 1869, spending most of his time treating sick freed-men in Washington, D.C. He was one of only six black physicians in the city. After four years of serving in the Union army, Dr. Charles Purvis was appointed to the medical faculty at Howard University. He became the second black teacher of medicine in the United States. The next fifty-seven years Purvis was a major influence at the Howard Medical School. He was known to be a real taskmaster that demanded his students and colleagues stay abreast of the latest medical innovations and developments. On July 2, 1881, when President Garfield was shot at the train station in Washington, Dr. Purvis was the first physician to arrive to treat the man. His highly skilled actions helped lead to his appointment later, as surgeon in chief of Freedmen's Hospital. Dr. Charles Purvis became the first African-American to head a civilian hospital.

Shirley Ann Jackson
Born: 1946

SHIRLEY ANN JACKSON

Dr. Jackson was recognized as a high achiever very early. Her family expected her to excel in school, and she did. Her mother made sure to expose her to the history of famous Africa-Americans and their accomplishments and her father helped with science projects for science fairs. "The Brain" as her young school friends called her, became the first African-American woman to earn a doctorate in physics. Shirley was born on August 5, 1946, in Washington, D.C. She was the second daughter of Beatrice and George Jackson. Unconcerned, neighbors thought of her as un-lady like, and too adventurous, Shirley collected dangerous insects and studied how they interacted with one another. Once when she found mold and fungi around her home, she turned it into a scientific investigation to determine the effect the growth of bacteria had on the environment. Her experiment won first place at a science fair. While she attended Roosevelt High School the teachers recognizing her potential, encouraged Shirley's passion to learn. At her high school graduation in 1964, she was valedictorian of her class. Shirley Jackson received an academic scholarship from Martin-Marietta Aircraft Company and a Prince Hall Mason Scholarship to support her college education. No one was surprised she became one of only fifteen African-America students that year to enroll at M.I.T., the prestigious Massachusetts Institute of Technology. College was initially, somewhat difficult for Shirley. White students avoided eating with her in the cafeteria and did not invite her to join their study groups, so she spent most of her studying time alone. However, during the second semester, she was chosen to be a laboratory assistant because of her excellence in difficult classes. Before long, other students began to ask her to tutor them. Feeling no longer isolated, she was confident she had what it took to succeed. When Shirley graduated with her Bachelor of Science degree in 1968, she received scholarship offers from Harvard University, the University of Chicago, and Brown University, etc. She chose to remain at M.I.T. for her graduate studies after learning her advisor would be Dr. James Young, M.I.T.'s first time tenured, or permanent African-American physics professor. At that time few, African-Americans were hired as science professors, and even fewer were tenured at the predominantly white universities. With funds from the Ford Foundation, Martin-Marietta, and the National Science Foundation, Shirley Jackson received her Ph.D. at age twenty-six. Dr. Shirley Jackson became a leading theoretical physicist. She explains her job as "trying to understand the interaction of the basic particles of matter." Her work was what's known as interacting physics where mathematics is used to study the "forces" holding together the nucleus of an atom. After receiving her doctorate, Dr. Shirley Jackson worked at the following famous laboratories, the Fermi National Accelerator Laboratory in Illinois, the European Center for Nuclear Research, and the AT&T Bell Laboratories in New Jersey. At AT&T Dr. Jackson studied semiconductors. Her work contributed to breakthroughs in many advanced communication systems. After sixteen years, Dr. Jackson was appointed to Rutgers University as a professor of physics. Along the way, Dr. Jackson married and had a son. She published more than a hundred scientific papers, and received countless awards. She became the head of the U.S. Nuclear Regulatory Commission protecting public health and safety in the nuclear age.

Francis Louis Cardozo
Born: 1837
Died: 1903

FRANCIS LOUIS CARDOZO

Francis Louis Cardozo was one of the leading black educators and political figures of the mid-1860s. He was born in Charleston, South Carolina February 1, 1837 to Jacob N. Cardozo a Jewish journalist and an economist, and a mother who was part black and Native American. Francis left school at twelve years old to learn a trade so he could eventually fulfill his dream of receiving an advanced education and becoming an ordained minister. Knowing there was no opportunity for him as a black student to receive advanced education in his state, Francis became a carpenter's apprentice for five years, and as a carpenter for four additional years. He worked hard to save his money to enroll in the University of Glasgow in Scotland. He supported himself by doing carpentry. Francis won a thousand dollar scholarship in a competitive examination given to Glasgow students and three other colleges. After studying in Glasgow for four years, he continued his studies at Presbyterian seminaries in Edinburgh and London for three more years. Then returning to the States during the Civil War in the 1864, Francis Cardozo became the pastor of the Temple Street Congregational Church in New Haven, Connecticut. He married Catherine Rowena Howell that year and eventually had six children. When the war ended in 1865, Francis Cardozo returned to Charleston, and with financial support of the American Missionary Association, established Avery Institute and begin his pioneering work in black education in the South. Initially, the Institute would only accommodate the earlier grades. Most of the students were from the city's free black population and already had some education. Cardozo hired twenty teachers, ten black and ten white. On the first day of school, there were more than a thousand students enrolled. Not long afterwards, Principal Cardozo introduced a more advance curriculum for the students including, classics, Latin, and higher mathematics. Avery Institute became one of the most successful schools in the South. In 1868, Francis Cardozo was elected a delegate to the state constitutional convention, a requirement under the Reconstruction Acts passed by the federal government. Cardozo served as chairman of the committee on education. And it was as chairman he was able to help plan a system of public schools for South Carolina, which his fellow delegates voted to approve. That same year, and again in 1870, he was elected South Carolina's secretary of state. Cardozo was the first African-American in the United States to be elected to a state cabinet office. He was elected state treasurer in 1872 and 1874. At the end of Reconstruction in 1877, came the return of white domination and the oppression that followed, ended Francis Cardozo's political career. He returned to Washington where he helped educate many more African-American students while serving as principal of the Colored Preparatory High School from 1884 to 1891. He also served as principal of the M Street High School from 1891 to 1896. After decades of working to improve the education of African-American children Francis Louis Cardozo died on July 22, 1903 in Washington. In 1928, a business high school in the nation's capital was named in his honor. His greatest legacy, is said to be the public school system he helped to establish in South Carolina and the countless children of all races who received an education because of his efforts.

Toni Morrison
Born: 1931
Died: 2019

TONI MORRISON

Toni Morrison is one of America's most celebrated and successful novelists. She is the first African-American to receive the Nobel Prize in 1993 for literature. As a storyteller, she compels her readers to remember those despicable terrors that have shaped American and African-American culture. The writer appears to be deeply concerned with the lifelong questions of love and death, the will to be free and the forces—both internal and external—that restrict that freedom. She was actually born Chloe Anthony Wofford to George and Rahmah Wofford on February 18, 1931, in Lorain, Ohio. Her family had been sharecroppers who had moved to Ohio after losing their land in Greenville, Alabama. Toni saw her parents as examples of black dignity and determination. She said her father distrusted "every word and every gesture of every white man on earth." She graduated with honors from Lorain High School, where she excelled in Latin. Toni studied English at Howard University where she makes a name change after receiving her B.A. degree in English in 1953. She then enrolled at Cornell where she earned a M.A. with a thesis on the theme of suicide in the works of William Faulkner and Virginia Woolf. In 1955, she taught at Southern University and then left to teach at Howard University from 1957 to 1964. Among Toni's students were a number of noted black activists. During this period of time she married architect Harold Morrison. The couple had two sons before their union ended. Before leaving Howard, Toni started to meet informally with a small group of poets and writers. Her first novel, The Bluest Eyes, was an idea that developed during that time. Resigning from Howard in 1964, Toni took a job as a textbook editor with Random House in Syracuse, and later relocated to New York City where until 1985, Toni continued to work as an editor for such African-American writers as Angela Davis, Toni Cade Bambara, Gayle Jones, and Muhammad Ali. Her editorship of The Black Book, an experimental collage of African-American history and literature was a major event in the world of African-American letters. She taught at Yale and the State University of New York at Purchase, and also held the prestigious Albert Schweitzer chair in the humanities at the State University of New York at Albany. She was the Robert F. Goheen Professor in the Humanities at Princeton, University. The following are a list of most of Toni Morrison's literary works: Bluest Eye (1969), Sula (1973), Song of Solomon (1977), Tar Baby (1981), Playing in the Dark (1992), Jazz (1992), Paradise (1997), Beloved (1987). "Her art beckons us to remember, endure, and prevail."

Colin Powell
Born: 1937
Died: 2021

COLIN POWELL

Colin Powell was born in Harlem in 1937, though his parents soon moved to the Bronx after his birth. Both parents were Jamaicans who had immigrated to America years before, and Powell owns to the complex bloodlines of many West Indians: African, English, Irish, Scottish, and possibly Arawak ancestry. Powell entered the City College of New York and its R.O.T.C. program in 1954. Though he was never a distinguished student before, Powell rose to the rank of cadet colonel, and became a second lieutenant in the army after graduating in 1958. He was sent to Germany for two years before returning to the U.S. Powell met and married his fiancé, Alma Johnson in 1962, with whom he later had three children. A few months after the wedding, he was sent to Vietnam. He served as an advisor to the South Vietnamese troops. After receiving injuries when he accidentally stepped on a punji stick, he received a Purple Heart for his distinctive performance while on duty. Shortly after the injury Powell returned to America. He wrote in his 1995, autobiography, My American Journey, that he was most struck by the conflict at home upon his return. His wife had been living with her parents in Birmingham, Alabama when the church bombing that killed four black girls made the troubles immediate; that's the date of his return, November 22, 1963, it coincided with the assassination of President John F. Kennedy filled him with despair. In his book, he wrote, "a world turned upside down." Powell spent the next few years preparing to advance upward in his military career. At Fort Benning's Infantry School, he performed admirably and was asked to be an instructor. In 1966, Powell became a major; then graduated second in his class at the United States Army Command and General Staff College before being sent back to Vietnam in 1968. On his second tour he worked on the staff of headquarters in the rear, though he was awarded the Purple Heart and the Soldier's Medal after rescuing men from a helicopter crash. Upon his return to the United States this time, his career went from just being an officer to an involvement in war politics. He obtained an MBA from George Washington University in 1971; White House fellow the following year; acceptance to the War College; commands of divisions around the world; senior military assistant to the Reagan's administration; National Security Advisor; four-star general; Chairman of the Joint Chiefs of Staff (and this is just an abridged resume). After Powell's retirement from the military, whenever he was called to give a speech, he always gave thanks to a country that had given him such opportunity. Colin Powell died in 2021.

Stevie Wonder
Born: 1950

STEVIE WONDER

Stevie Wonder was actually born Stevland Hardaway Morris on May 13, 1950 to Lula Mae Hardaway. He did not have an easy childhood growing up without a father in one of Detroit, Michigan's poorest neighborhoods. Born blind from birth Stevie lived in a world of sounds. When the boy began to bang on anything he got his hands on, his mother bought him a set of cardboard drums. She knew sound was important to him. The boy would spend hours listening to the radio. The blues was what he loved best, especially if it was Ray Charles. He knew his favorite artist shared something in common. Ray Charles was also blind. Stevie decided to be a musician like idol. He took lessons in classical piano and learned to play a number of other instruments. Stevie's new musical skills were practiced on his friends and family to entertain as his audience. By the time he was ten years old he was writing his own songs. After Stevie met Ronnie White who was part of the popular singing group known as the Miracles, he was introduced at the black owned Motown Record Company. People there loved his music so much they signed the child prodigy with Motown's Tamla label at age eleven. "Little Stevie Wonder" became his professional name. His first record "Fingertips" a single was made in 1963. It became a number-one hit on the Billboard Hot 100 when he was thirteen, making him the youngest artist ever to top the chart. Stevie Wonder's success was at its peak in the 1970s. He wrote hit after hit and became one of the most successful song writers and musicians. He was virtually a one-man band during those peak years. His use of synthesizers and electronic musical instruments during the 1970s helped expand the sound of R&B. He is also credited as one of the artists who helped drive R&B into the album era by crafting his LPs as cohesive, consistent statements with complex sounds. He was best known for his harmonica work in his childhood, but is best known now for his keyboard skills and vocal ability. Stevie Wonder also plays the piano, synthesizer, congas, drums, bongos, organ, melodica and Clavinet. On August 6, 1973, He was injured in a serious automobile accident while on tour in North Carolina. He was left in a coma for four days that resulted in a partial loss of his sense of smell and a temporary loss of taste. Despite the orders from his doctor not to perform, Stevie Wonder performed at a homecoming benefit for Shaw University in Raleigh. The University was facing financial difficulties, so as a member of the school's board of trustees, he rallied other acts to join the concert, which raised over $10,000 for the school's scholarship fund. He is also noted for his work as an activist for political causes, including his 1980 campaign to make Martin Luther King, Jr's birthday a federal holiday in the U.S. In 2009, he was named the United Nations Messenger of Peace, and in 2014, he was honored with the Presidential Medal of Freedom.

George Washington Williams
Born: 1849
Died: 1891

GEORGE WASHINGTON WILLIAMS

Three years after the Civil War had started in 1861, young George Washington Williams then fifteen, enlisted in the Union Army. He was one of the youngest men to fight in the war between the Northern and Southern states. He had been rejected before for being too young. George decided to lie about his age and registered again in Meadville, a different city where he registered as William Seward. There is no knowledge of his parents being aware before-hand of his attempts to join the army. His father was a minister and a barber who traveled a lot, and his mother worked outside of the home. The youngster was left often on his own. Williams was born on October 16, 1849 in Bedford Springs, Pennsylvania. Williams served for a time with the Tenth Army Corps, commanded by Major General D. B. Birney. According to Williams, he was wounded in September 1864 when the Army Corps was in an assault on Fort Harrison, near Richmond, Virginia. After a quick recovery, he returned to fight. When all the black troops became the U.S. Colored Troops, Williams was assigned to the Second Division of the Twenty-fifth Army Corps. He and his fellow troops engaged in battle at Hatcher's Run, Five Forks, and along the sixteen-battle line to Petersburg, Virginia. On April 2, 1865, the Confederate Army surrendered, and the twenty-fifth Army Corps went to Texas. Shortly, Williams returned home to Pennsylvania but, with no formal education or marketable skills, there were few job opportunities. And the U.S. Army had taken few steps in securing a permanent place for African-American soldiers who had fought in the Civil War, So young Williams left the army and crossed the Texas border into Mexico where he joined the Mexican General Espinosa's army against the French. He was given a commission as lieutenant and served until the spring of 1867. Before the final march of victory over the French, Williams returned to the United States. He then went to Pittsburgh and enlisted five more years in the Twenty-seventh Infantry, under the command of Captain H. Haymond. Assigned as a drill sergeant, he helped to recruit one hundred new men, and deliver them to Fort Riley, Kansas. Williams and the new recruits were assigned to the Indian Territory with the Tenth Cavalry. He assisted in the rebuilding of Fort Arbuckle and protecting the settlers on the frontier. Williams received a gunshot wound to a lung May 19, 1868 and was hospitalized for the remainder of his time in the service. He had not reached nineteen, but his career was over. Upon being discharged on September 4, 1868, the Army presented him with a Certificate of Disability. William began his study for the ministry, initially in St. Louis, Missouri, then at Howard University in Washington, D.C. Eventually, he enrolled a Newton Theological Institution (now Seminary),in Newton, Massachusetts. He was the first African-American to graduate from that seminary in 1874. That year Williams married Sarah Sterrett and became a minister at Watertown, Massachusetts. He served as pastor for many years at Twelfth Street Baptist Church in Boston. Before he and his wife divorced in 1886 the couple had a son. Williams then moved to Washington, D.C. where he started a newspaper, The Commoner. He then left to be minister of Union Baptist Church and to write for local publications in Cincinnati, Ohio. He stated to read law, and was admitted to the Ohio bar in 1879. That year he campaigned and won the election for State House of Representatives from Hamilton, County. Williams became Ohio's first black state legislator. While in Ohio, Williams took an interest in African-American history and became a voracious reader. In 1883, he published a two-volume study entitled History of the Negro Race in America from 1619 to 1880. Five years later, he published his History of Negro Troops in the War of Rebellion, 1861-1865, making him the first major African-American historian. After Williams visited the Congo in Africa, he wrote a crucial article against colonialism, and served as a U.S. diplomat in Haiti from 1885-1886. Later, Williams moved to England, where he did research. He died in 1891 from a mysterious illness.

Dorothy Vaughan
Born: 1910
Died: 2008

DOROTHY VAUGHAN

Dorothy Vaughan was born in Kansas City, Missouri in 1910. When she was two years old, her mother died. Later, her father remarried. Her stepmother took a great interest in her education and encouraged her to do well in school. She taught Dorothy how to read before she began school. When Dorothy was eight the family moved to West Virginia. Dorothy did so well in high school, she became valedictorian of her class. The African Methodist Episcopal Sunday School Convention issued her a four year scholarship to Wilberforce University, the country's oldest black college. Her grades were so good in mathematics, a professor recommended her for graduate study in mathematics at Howard University in Washington, D.C. Dorothy aware there was a Depression and her parents were struggling to make ends meet, she did not accept the opportunity to go to graduate school. She decided to get a job to help support her family. After graduation in 1929, Dorothy looked for a job as a math and English teacher. The rural jobs where she taught soon closed their doors due to the lingering effects of the Depression. During the spring of 1943, she saw a federal agency bulletin advertising in Hampton, Virginia for women to fill mathematical positions at a facility specializing in the development of airplanes. At first glance, Dorothy assumed those jobs were for the white well-to-do students from the State Teachers College in Farmville. It never occurred to her that the Langley Memorial Aeronautical Laboratory would accept an application from an African-American woman. But during World II, the United States was asking all of its citizens of every ethnic background, women as well as men to apply. In the first week in May, 1943, the Norfolk Journal and Guide published the article "Pave the Way for Women Engineers". It caught her eye. Dorothy thought maybe there was a place for African-American women who loved working with numbers. Though she decided to fill out an application, Dorothy was concerned about leaving her husband and children for long periods. She reasoned if she were accepted, it would certainly be an opportunity of a lifetime. She would be able to save for her children's education. So when she saw the question on the application that asked, "How soon could you be ready to start work?" Dorothy responds she could be ready in forty-eight hours. In December 1943, Dorothy began working for NACA's West Area Computing unit, a group of Africa-American women mathematicians who were considered "human computers," performing complex computations and analyzing data for aerospace engineers. The West Computers, as the women were known, provided data that were later essential to the success of the early U.S. space program. Dorothy loved her new job in Hampton, and was proud to be helping her country in its war efforts. But she missed her family terribly. Often working eighteen hour days and meeting job demands made it difficult to get home except during holidays. At that time, the company was segregated, and the black employees were forced to use separate dining and bathroom facilities. Dorothy Vaughan was promoted to lead the West Computers in 1949, despite the conditions. She became NACA's first black supervisor. She served as head of the West Computes until 1958, when NACA incorporated into the newly created NASA, which closed the segregated facilities. Dorothy Vaughan and many other West Computers joined NASA's Analysis and Computation Division, a group made up of men and women of all races. By then, the space program had begun using electronic computers, and Dorothy became an expert at FORTRAN, a computer programming language used for scientific and algebraic applications. In 1971, Dorothy retired from NASA.

Mary Jackson
Born: 1921
Died: 2005

MARY JACKSON

Mary Jackson was born Mary Winston in Hampton, Virginia on April 9, 1921. She went to school there, and in 1938 graduated from Phenix High School with highest honors. She then enters Hamilton Institute where most female students earned degrees in home economics or nursing, but Mary studied math and physical science. After graduating she accepted a teaching position in Maryland until she returned home a year later, to help care for her ailing dad. Back in Hamilton she began working for a community center run by the United Services Organization (USO), a nonprofit group that provided different services to the United States soldiers. Mary helped military families and defense workers find living accommodations. She also helped organize Girl Scout troop meetings and rallies, and played the piano during sing-alongs. Eventually, Mary got married. When World War II ended, the USO shut down, and Mary found a new job as a bookkeeper briefly, but left after the birth of her son. While the care of her son kept her busy, she always found time for activities that made her happy. One of the things she loved most was leading Girl Scout Troop II, which was associated with her church. The organization embodied Mary's core beliefs of committing to preparing women to take their place in the world with a mission of respect for God and country, and of honesty and loyalty. Understanding how impressionable young girls are, Mary exposed them to various positive learning experiences and adventures. Once at one of the troop meetings a song was chosen. In the midst of singing the song, Mary interrupted everyone and said, "We are never going to sing this song again." She explained that it reinforced all the worst stereotypes about what it meant to be black. She said they could be much more. Mary believed even if she could not remove the limits that society put on girls, it was her duty to try to make sure they did not put limits on themselves. Their skin color, their gender, their economic status: none of these were reasons not live out their dreams. For Mary Jackson, life was a long process of raising one's expectations. After Mary's son turned four, she put an application in with the Civil Service for both a secretarial position and a job as a computer at Langley. In 1951 Mary was hired a secretary at Fort Monroe, an army base in Hampton. After the history of her background in mathematics surfaced, the government offered her a job working at Langley. She then resigned from the army base and went to work for Dorothy Vaughan the lead West Computer. Mary started working at the National Advisory Committee for Aeronautics (NACA), where she was a member of its West Area Computing unit: the West Computers, comprising of black female mathematicians and the supervisor Dorothy Vaughan. At the time, the (NACA) was segregated, Black employees were had to use separate bathrooms and dining facilities. In 1953, Mary Jackson left the West Computer to work for engineer Kakimierz Czarnecki, conducting experiments in a high-speed wind tunnel. Her boss suggested that she should enter a training program that would allow her to become an engineer. Because Virginia schools were still segregated, Mary had to get special permission to take classes with white students. After meeting all the necessary requirements, in 1958, Mary became the first Black female engineer at NASA. Mary Jackson worked as an aerospace engineer for twenty years. Much of her work centered around the airflow around aircraft. Despite early promotions, she was denied management-level jobs, so she left engineering in 1979 and took a demotion to become manager of the women's program at NASA. In that position she set out to improve the opportunities for all women in the organization. Mary retired in 1985.

John Hope Franklin
Born: 1915
Died: 2009

JOHN HOPE FRANKLIN

John Hope Franklin is said to be the person most responsible for conferring academic legitimacy on the study of black history. He made it inexcusable for any history of America to ever again omit the history of African-Americans. He was born January 2, 1915 and raised in the town of Rentiesville, Oklahoma. His father was a lawyer and his mother was a school teacher. John's father worked as a lawyer in the city of Tulsa in 1921 when the deadly riot broke-out and his father barely escaped. Hearing firsthand accounts from his father of the rioting that killed over a hundred blacks, was a lesson in racism that haunted the boy's childhood. John attended Fisk University where he earned high honors and a bachelor's degree in history in 1935. John applied to Harvard University for graduate school at the suggestion of his history professor. He earned his master's there in 1936, then a doctorate in 1941. After being rejected by the local army when he tried entering in World War II, John Franklin spent a few years teaching at black institutions, including Fist and Howard Universities. In 1956, John Franklin was appointed chair of the history department at Brooklyn College. A black person obtaining a chair position at a white institution in the United States at the time, was thought to be an extraordinary breakthrough. Though outwardly, he found in his situation racism was less blatant in the North, but just as inhospitable as Jim Crow in South. "You could vote," he later recalled. Despite his position as head of the all-white fifty-two-person department, John Franklin faced entrenched racism and had to engage over a hundred realtors before finding one willing to sell him a house. John Franklin remained at Brooklyn eight years, then eighteen at the University of Chicago, again as chair of the history Department. His book, From Slavery to Freedom: A History of American Negroes, first published in 1947. His work earned him a reputation as the actual successor to historians W.E.B. Du Bois and Carter G. Woodson (both Harvard Ph. D.s in history). NAACP Chairman Roy Wilkins wrote that John Franklin has consistently corrected the misinformation of this country's rich heritage. His book has sold over three million copies and is still widely used. Another one of John Franklin's ground breaking works written in 1943, The Free Negro in North Carolina, 1790-1860, was one of the first books to uncover the history of black Americans outside the institution of slavery. His other projects research the birth of Jim Crow and other aspects of American racial inequality. In addition to his John Franklin's academic involvement, he conducted research for Thurgood Marshall the during the 1954 landmark case Brown v. Board of Education, which ended legal segregation in public schools. He marched with Martin Luther King, Jr. in Washington, D.C. in 1963 and in Selma in 1965. Though John Hope Franklin retired in 1992, he continued his writing projects. John Franklin received the Presidential Medal of Freedom in 1996.

Muhammad Ali
Born: 1942
Died: 2021

MUHAMMAD ALI

Muhammad Ali was given the name Cassius Marcellus Clay, Jr. at birth by his parents Cassius and Odessa Clay. His father painted signs and his mother worked as a domestic. While Clay was not a very good student in high school, and was later rejected by the army when he scored quite low on their assessment. It is reported his response to the army was, "I never said I was the smartest. I said I was the greatest." Even though he may have graduated at the low end of his graduating class, he was ferociously intelligent. At the early age of twelve, Clay began boxing under the guidance of policeman Joe Martin, who helped him appear in 108 bouts between 1955 and 1960. At which time, he won six Kentucky Golden Gloves titles, his first novice one at fourteen, two national Amateur Athletic Union championships, and two National Golden Gloves crowns. By eighteen, Clay had won a gold medal in the light heavyweight division in the 1960 Summer Olympic Games in Rome. After returning to the U.S. and signing a promotional contract with a sponsoring group in Louisville, he met his trainer Angelo Dundee. He made his debut fight as a heavyweight in October 1960 with a six-round decision over boxer Tunney Hunsaker. Boasting and bragging, he won his following eighteen fights, fifteen by knockouts. Before his sixth professional bout against Lamar Clark on April 19, 1961, Clay predicted a second-round knockout. He turned out to be right, and continued making predictions in rhyme, and making them a reality until March 13, 1963. On that date, he won a questionable ten-round decision over Doug Jones after making his prediction Jones would be knockout in the fourth. Clay was not the greatest until he fought Sonny Liston on February 25, 1964, in Miami Beach, Florida. Before that Liston reigned as the heavyweight champion. Liston a hardened boxer, managed by organized crime, had easily knocked out his last three opponents in the first round. Hardly any of his challengers reached the fifth round. The press annoyed with Clay's boasting, predicted he would be the loser. Weeks before the fight, twenty-two year old Clay publicly threatened Liston with words. A shock for the press any many others came when Clay actually defeats Sonny Liston. Days later, Clay announced to the world he had converted to the Nation of Islam, and his name was no longer Cassius Clay, but Muhammad Ali. The shocking revelation of his embrace of black nationalism, resulting from his association with Malcom X alienated the press. The New York Times refused to acknowledge his new name when writing about him throughout the sixties. In 1965, Ali won the Sonny Liston rematch held in Lewiston, Maine. He defended his title a second time that same year against Floyd Patterson. In 1966, Ali was drafted by the Army. He refused to fight in the Vietnam War and explained his reason for being a conscientious objector, "I ain't got no quarrel with them Viet Cong." After completing a speech, he is fined ten thousand dollars and sentenced five years in prison. Then Muhammad Ali is stripped of his heavyweight title and license to box in 1967. However, the Supreme Court reversed the decision, granting him conscientious objector status. In 1970, Ali came back with knockout victories over Jerry Quarry and Oscar Bonavena, and lost the first time to Joe Frazier March 8, 1971. Nevertheless, he did regain his championship status on October 30, 1974 after his "Rumble in the Jungle" in Kinshasa, Zaire (now the Democratic Republic of the Congo) with George Foreman. Zaire Ali was hailed as a Pan-African hero. Among Ali Muhammad's greatest fights were his victory over Frazier on October 1, 1975, in Manilla, Philippines, promoted as the "Thriller in Manilla" and the February 15, 1978, match in Las Vegas, Nevada, when he lost the crown to Olympic Champion Leon Spinks which he regained in 1978. After retiring from boxing, Ali develop Parkinson's disease in the late 1980s. Before his illness, he created the Muhammad Ali Community and Economic Development Corporation to teach job skills to low-income public housing residents in Chicago.

Angela Davis
Born: 1944

ANGELA DAVIS

Angela Davis is known as a crusader for social justice. In the 1960s and 70s her name triggered the images of defiant protests-fists raised in black power salutes and proud natural hairstyles that were symbols of a young people's march toward freedom. That seemed to be an era in which many were overcome by a sense of hopelessness. It was through the politics of the 1960s that Davis became best known. Her defiant image graced the FBI's most-wanted posters. She became a black power icon. Her roots in social justice activism went much deeper than the charged events. She was one of four siblings whose parents were teachers. Her father bought a gas station and relocated his family to Birmingham, Alabama. The neighborhood Davis grew up in was called "Dynamite Hill" because it was periodically a bombing target for white supremacists. She attended all-black public schools where she was exposed to African-American history early on, which instilled in her a sense of confidence and pride. She often went to civil rights demonstrations with her mother as a young girl. But the local police would break up the interracial study groups that Davis tried to organize with friends on her own. She was sent to Elizabeth Irwin High in New York's Greenwich Village, a private magnet school for budding activists. The political ideology of most of the school's teachers left them unable to find work with any public systems. Davis graduated in 1961, then attended Brandeis University where she majored in French Literature. In Paris, she met African students who had grown up under colonial regimes. She felt there was a connection between their struggles and her own in the United States; the stories of their experiences increased her resolve for social change. Angela returned to Brandeis seeking through her academic work a plausible political philosophy that could end injustice against African-Americans. After an introduction to Marxism by her professor at Brandeis, she believed she had found a way to understand and change the structural conditions of racism in the States, and oppressed groups the world over. In 1965, Angela graduated with highest honors and started graduate work at the University of Frankfurt in Germany. As the racial unrest at home escalated, Angela felt she had to return. She finished her master's at the University of California at San Diego, began doctorial work, and got involved in the Student Nonviolent Coordinating Committee and the Black Panther Party. Angela began an association with the Communist party during which she ran on the party's ticket for vice president in 1980 and 1984. Though Angela was hired as an assistant professor of philosophy at UCLA in 1969, her Communist membership caused an overflow of concern by the school's Board of Regents. Under the leadership of then Governor Reagan, they attempted to fire her. After protests coming from faculty and students, Angela was reinstated by court order. However, she was not reinstated the next year when her contract expired. Angela began working with prisoners and prison activists. She offered help to the Soledad members, a Marxist group, when one of their men was murdered by a guard and ruled "justified homicide" by the warden. At the courthouse an attempted high-stake rescue ensued resulting in a shootout that left a judge dead. The weapons used were traced to Angela. She went underground until captured in New York, then extradited to California and jailed for sixteen months before her case went to trial. She was charged with murder, conspiracy and kidnapping in connection with the courthouse shooting. Though acquitted of all charges in 1972 after months of worldwide protests during a period she called" the most painful years of her life", She later promoted the ideas of multicultural coalitions and global strategies to achieve equality and end racism and oppression. She says "It is no longer possible for various groups to live and function and struggle in isolation." Angela Davis founded the National Alliance Against Racism and Political Repression. Her books include, Angela Davis: An Autobiography; Women, Race and Class; Women, Culture & Politics.

BIBLIOGRAPHY

Beckner, Chrisanne. 100 African Americans Who Shaped American History. Blue Wood Books. San Mateo, CA. 1995.

Blackwell, Sandra T. Westchester County Mourns Loss of Dr. Olivia J. Hooker. The Westchester County Press. November 29, 2018.

Cox, Clinton. Black Stars of Civil War Times. John Wiley and Son, Inc. New Jersey, 2003

Falstein, Mark. Meeting the Challenge: Biographies of Black Americans. The Continental Press, Inc. Elizabethtown, Pennsylvania. 1987.

Gates, Jr. Henry Louis, et al. The African-American Century: How Black Americans Have Shaped Our Country. Simon and Schuster. New York, N. Y. 2002.

Krensky, Stephen. Biography Barack Obama. DK Publishing. New York. 2010.

Lanker, Brian. I Dream A World: Portraits of Black Women Who Changed American. Stewart, Tabori &Chang A Division of U.S. Media Holdings, Inc. New York, N.Y. 1999.

Madyun, Julian B. EMANCIPATION: It's about time you got the whole picture!!! Mandela Publishing. Decatur, GA. 2000.

Schraff, Anne. Marcus Garvey: Controversial Champion of Black Pride. Enslow Publishers, Inc. Berkley, Heights, New Jersey.

Shetterly, Margot Lee. HIDDEN FIGURES, Young Readers' Edition. Harper Collins Publishers. New York, N.Y. 2016.

Sullivan, Otha Richard. Black Stars: African American Inventors. John Wiley and Sons, Inc. New York, N.Y. 1998.

Sullivan, Otha Richard. Black Stars: African American Women Scientists and Inventors. John Wiley and Sons, Inc. New York, N.Y. 2002.

ADDITIONAL RESEARCH RECOMMENDATIONS

Historical Figures
Peter Salem
Pedro Alonzo Nino
Nat Turner

Leaders and Politicians
James Farmer
Julian Bond
Roy Wilkins
Patricia Harris
Edward Brooke

Educators
Marva Collins
Benjamin Mays
Daniel James, Jr.
Samuel Gravely
Elizabeth Koontz

Business
Thomas Burrell
Robert Abbott
Andrew Brimmer
Arthur Gaston
Samuel Cornish

Sports
Cheryl Miller
Warren Moon

Scientists and Inventors
Meredith Gourdine
Michael Croslin
Earl D. Shaw
Henry Blair
William Hinton

Writers
James Baldwin
Aaron Douglass
Alice Walker
Countee Cullen
William Brown

Music, Singers, Composers
Count Basie
Duke Ellington
Lionel Hampton
Mahalia Jackson
W.C. Handy

Actors and Dancers
Alvin Ailey
Diana Carroll
Gregory Hines

www.ingramcontent.com/pod-product-compliance
Lightning Source LLC
Chambersburg PA
CBHW081348070526
44578CB00005B/772